FANTASTIC
WORLD OF
BIRDS

FANTASTIC
WORLD OF
BIRDS

MARTIN WALTERS

PUBLISHING

First published in 2000 by Miles Kelly Publishing Ltd
Bardfield Centre
Great Bardfield
Essex CM7 4SL

24681097531

ISBN 1902947290

Design   Jo Brewer
Cover Design   GardnerQuainton
Page Make-up   Helen Weller
Editor   Steve Parker
Production   Rachel Jones
Research & Index   Jane Parker

Art Director   Clare Sleven
Editorial Director   Paula Borton
Director   Jim Miles

The publishers wish to thank Ted Smart
for the generous loan of his illustrations.
Illustrators include Jim Channell, John Francis,
Robert Morton and Colin Newman.

Printed in Hong Kong

Contents

World of birds

▶ Within the pages of this book all the animals shown in the main picture are listed in this panel. They are named in alphabetical order.

Mute swan
All (or most) of the animals pictured in this book have their own entries, giving important details about their lifestyles, where they live, what they eat and how they breed.

Birds are the only creatures that benefit from feathers. They are delicate yet strong. They keep in body warmth, give protection, create camouflage to hide the bird in its surroundings, and produce bright colours and patterns for mates at breeding time.

Feathers also form a large wing area for flight and a smooth, streamlined body covering. Different birds can fly faster than an arrow, straighter than a bullet, hover like a helicopter, flutter, swerve, dive into the water and swim underneath.

There are more than 8600 kinds of birds. They live in hot deserts, thick forests and the open ocean.

You will always find a strange or amazing fact in this panel!

Biggest are the flightless ostriches, taller than a person. Smallest are hummingbirds, almost as tiny as a fingertip. In between are the fastest living thing – the peregrine falcon in its 'stoop' power-dive – and one of the most common and useful animals on our planet, the farmyard hen.

The world of birds is far more exotic than chickens. There are sakers, boobies, frigates, choughs, phoebes, motmots, bulbuls, todies, shags and potoos – to name just a few. This book describes where they live, what they eat and much more. And why some birds, sadly, need our help – because we have almost made them extinct.

Too big to fly

The world's largest and most unusual birds live on the open grassland and scrub of the southern continents. They cannot fly – their wings are too small and their bodies are too big and heavy. They are the ostrich of Africa, the emu of Australia and the rhea of South America. They are tall and strong with powerful back legs, and they can run rapidly from danger or kick and slash enemies. The cassowary and kiwi skulk in dark, dense forests. All of these flightless birds lay large eggs. In the ostrich, emu and rhea several females put their eggs in one nest and the male guards them. The chicks huddle together into a small flock as soon they hatch.

Rhea
Smaller than the ostrich and emu, the rhea is still the largest bird in the Americas. It roams the pampas (grassland), often gathering in large flocks of a hundred or more birds. At breeding time the male rhea gathers a group or harem of up to a dozen females, then digs a hole for them to lay their eggs.

Emu
The emu is almost as large as the ostrich, at nearly 2 m tall. These big, tough birds live in many parts of Australia, where they feed mainly on grasses, fruits, flowers and seeds. Emus are usually on the move. They search the dry outback for an area where it has recently rained and plants are growing.

Bennet's cassowary
This type of cassowary is about 100 cm tall. It has a fearsome reputation as a very dangerous bird. It may attack anything or anyone who comes too close to its nest, kicking out with the sharp claw on each foot. These birds live in scrub and bushy country in the mountains of New Guinea.

Cassowary
Found in parts of northern Australia and New Guinea, the cassowary has colourful, turkey-like wattles (flaps of skin) hanging from its head and neck. To attract a female at breeding time the male shows off these wattles. He also balloons out his throat pouch to make strange, deep, booming sounds.

Kiwi
Symbol of New Zealand, the kiwi is well known yet seldom seen. Its feathers are so thin and fine that the bird looks like a ball of fur. Kiwis creep about in the forest at night, pecking and poking in the soil for worms and grubs. Compared to its body size the kiwi's egg is the largest of any bird.

Ostrich
The ostrich is the tallest (2.5 m), heaviest (150 kg) and fastest-running (40 km/h) of all birds. Ostriches favour the dry savanna (grassland) of Africa and survive well on a wide variety of foods, from seeds to lizards and frogs. The male shades the eggs and chicks from the scorching sun with his plume-like wing feathers.

The ostrich lays the largest eggs of any bird. Yet compared to the size of the mother bird they are the smallest eggs of any bird. Biggest are the kiwi's (see above).

Flightless birds

Expert swimmers of southern seas

Penguins cannot fly. But they certainly can swim. They are the fastest and most skilled swimmers of all birds. A penguin spends hours each day diving under the ocean waves to chase food such as fish, squid, prawns and the small, shrimp-like animals known as krill. The penguin's paddle-shaped wings flap up and down as they would do in air, to 'fly' through the water. Penguins live mainly on rocky islands and icebergs around Antarctica. On land they walk with an awkward, upright waddle or 'toboggan' on their chests. But in water the webbed feet and short tail work as rudders so the penguin can twist and turn with tremendous speed and grace.

10

Gentoo penguin
Gentoos feed largely on krill. In years when the krill are scarce, as part of their natural population cycle, gentoos may not try to breed at all.

Yellow-eyed penguin
Found as far north as New Zealand, this is one of the rarest penguins. It nests in isolated pairs rather than in large groups or colonies.

Adelie penguin
These are the most southerly penguins. They breed on the cold coasts of Antarctica itself, during the brief summer when the water is ice-free.

Little blue penguin
This is the smallest penguin, only 40 cm tall. Most penguins feed by day but the little blue does so at dusk, bringing food back to its nest burrow in the dark.

Magellanic penguin
These penguins live as far north as Chile and Brazil. Their breeding sites echo by day with noisy shrieking calls. At night they hide in their burrows and all is quiet.

Emperor penguin
The largest penguin, at 1.2 m tall, is also the heaviest seabird. Each male holds his partner's single egg on his feet for some 60 days until the chick hatches.

Royal penguin
Royals live mainly on Macquarie Island, south of New Zealand. They number more than one million birds. Half of these live in a single huge colony.

Rockhopper penguin
The rockhopper jumps with great skill around its stony breeding sites, on the bare and remote islands near Antarctica.

Chinstrap penguin
Named after the dark line on its chin, this the most numerous penguin. Its large colonies total several million birds.

The gentoo penguin is the fastest bird swimmer, speeding along under the water at 27 km/h – five times faster than a person. Some penguins dive down to depths of 250 m.

Life on the ocean wave

12

'Tube-noses' are birds who spend almost their whole lives soaring over the open ocean. This odd name comes from the position of their nostrils (breathing openings). These are not at the base of the beak just below the eyes, as in most birds, but part-way along the beak at the end of tube-like extensions. The group includes petrels, fulmars, shearwaters and the bird with the longest wings in the world – the wandering albatross. They glide and soar in all weathers, even over mountainous waves in howling gales. These birds feed by swooping down and snatching fish, squid and other food from the surface, using their long, sharp, down-hooked beaks.

Light-mantled sooty albatross

There are 14 kinds of albatrosses. This is one of the smallest with wings about 1.5 m across. It lives in the far south around Antarctica. Unlike other albatrosses, which make untidy nests or none at all, the female and male build a tidy, bowl-shaped nest from bits of plants. They rear a single chick.

Wandering albatross

You can watch a wandering albatross for hours and never see it flap its wings. It glides quite low, usually less than 20 m above the waves, where rising winds keep it aloft. Albatrosses learned the trick of following ships for thrown-away food scraps, so they feature in many sailors' tales.

Manx shearwater

This common seabird is found around the Pacific and Atlantic Oceans and in the Mediterranean Sea. It wanders widely over the ocean for weeks on each feeding trip, covering up to 500 km each day. Then it returns to its breeding colony where thousands of these shearwaters nest in burrows.

Leach's storm petrel

Storm petrels are among the smallest seabirds, many measuring less than 20 cm from beak to tail. Yet they can fly even in the worst storms, or sit on the sea as giant waves crash around them. Leach's storm petrel lives in northern oceans and feeds by swooping near to the water's surface.

Wilson's storm petrel

Storm petrels of southern oceans, like Wilson's, often feed by swooping down and then 'stepping' on the ocean surface. They seem to run or hop along as they stab with their beaks for small food items like krill. These petrels only come to land during the breeding season.

Fulmar

This large, strong, gull-like petrel has become common because it feeds on scraps from fishing boats and bullies other birds away from this food. Like other tube-noses the fulmar keeps a store of food in its stomach, in the form of thick oil. If a predator comes near the bird vomits up the oil as a foul-smelling spray!

The wings of the wandering albatross can measure 3.2 m from tip to tip. Wilson's storm petrel is one of the five commonest birds in the world.

Albatrosses and petrels

Ocean soarers and divers

Many birds of the open sea have stretchy, balloon-like throat pouches which they use to scoop up fish. Pelicans are among the largest and heaviest of these ocean soarers (see also page 16). They are clumsy on land and walk with an awkward waddle. But in the air they glide without effort on their broad wings, using winds and rising air currents (thermals) to stay aloft. Gannets also soar over the sea in flocks. When they spot a shoal of fish just below the surface they fold their wings back and plunge like arrows into the water to feed. Frigatebirds and tropicbirds are graceful gliders and spend days at a time soaring over the world's warmer oceans.

Frigatebird

Frigatebirds nest on islands in tropical seas. With their long, narrow, angled-back wings and deeply forked tails, they are exceptionally graceful and skilled fliers. They can glide slowly and also beat their wings rapidly to fly against gale-force winds. Frigatebirds sometimes use their speed to chase other seabirds and make them drop their food, which the frigatebird then eats. The male has a red balloon-like pouch on his neck. He inflates this to attract the white-fronted female during breeding time.

Red-tailed tropicbird

The most distinctive feature of the beautiful tropicbird is its tail streamers, formed by narrow, extra-long central tail feathers. The feathers may measure up to 50 cm in length. Tropicbirds spend most of their time on the wing over the open sea, watching for fish, squid, shrimps and similar creatures just below the surface. They catch their food by hovering and diving onto it in a flurry of spray. Tropicbirds breed on rocky cliffs and outcrops on ocean islands – the only time they come to land.

Australian gannet

Gannets are powerful, ocean-going seabirds which usually feed in flocks. They glide and soar over the waves, watching for fish below. When the flock finds a shoal, the gannets go into a frenzy of dive-bombing as bird after bird drops into the sea, emerging with a fish in its beak. To help this plunge-dive method of feeding the gannet's body with its wings folded back is shaped like a torpedo, and its beak is long and sharply pointed. In tropical regions most types of gannets are known as boobies.

American white pelican

This pelican is a gregarious or social bird, which means it is nearly always seen in flocks with others of its kind. The flock usually rests on seashore rocks or on a sandbar. Then they take off with a whirlwind of wingbeats to settle on the sea nearby and scoop up large pouchfuls of water and fish. The pouch is made smaller to spill out the water and leave the food, which the pelican swallows. These birds are also found on inland lakes, where they make big, untidy nests from sticks, waterweeds and stones.

The Australian pelican has the longest beak of any bird – up to 47 cm.

Pelicans and similar seabirds

Birds of shores and shallows

16

In addition to waders and gulls, many other types of birds can be seen fishing or foraging along the sea coast, or diving for food in the shallows. Cormorants and shags, with their dark plumage, are often spotted on shores, estuaries and harbours, and also on inland lakes well stocked with fish. Like their cousins the pelicans, they have stretchy, balloon-like throat pouches. The cormorant swims below the surface after its prey with amazing speed and agility. However its feathers become waterlogged. This helps the bird to stay under the water. But it also means that, after its meal, the cormorant must sit for a long time with its wings held out to dry.

Darter
Sometimes called the snakebird because of its long and bendy neck, the darter is an expert fish-catcher. It lives on rivers and lakes and uses its sharp, dagger-like beak to spear fish underwater. The darter swims low in the water, often with just the head and neck visible – which also makes it look like a snake.

Brown pelican
Unlike other pelicans, the brown pelican feeds from the air. It soars about 15 m high over the water, then folds its wings and plunge-dives to catch a fish in its chin pouch. Brown pelicans are found along the coasts of North and South America and also around the Caribbean and Galapagos Islands.

Pied cormorant
Like most cormorants, the pied cormorant of Australia and New Zealand nests in large colonies. It sometimes gathers in flocks of thousands.

Atlantic shag
Looking like a small cormorant, the shag has beautiful, glossy, dark green feathers. It prefers rocky coasts and breeds in small colonies on cliff ledges.

Red-billed tropicbird
Rocky ledges on tropical islands are the main breeding sites of these birds. They spend most of their time gliding over the open sea, rarely landing except to breed.

Dalmatian pelican
Some pelicans are fairly common but the Dalmatian pelican is on the official list of threatened species. Only about 2000 survive on lakes in eastern Europe and across Russia to China. The pelican likes shallow water – but so do people, for fishing and boating. They easily disturb this timid bird.

Red- and blue-footed boobies
Boobies are open-ocean birds that plunge-dive for fish, like their close relatives the gannets. The red-footed booby is common over tropical oceans. Unlike its cousins it nests in trees rather than on ledges or the ground. Blue-footed boobies breed on the Galapagos Islands of the East Pacific.

Cormorants, pelicans and similar seabirds

Standing tall in the water

18

The 60 different kinds (species) of herons are found around the world. Most are grey or brown but some smaller types, known as egrets, are pure white. The storks, with about 17 species, are similar to herons – tall birds with long legs and long beaks. Herons prefer marshes and lakes while most storks stride across grassland and scrub. All of these birds feed on small animals which they catch on the ground. They are slow but graceful in the air. Herons tuck in their long necks when flying, storks hold their necks stretched out straight. Spoonbills and ibises are also tall birds that mainly wade in water, feeling for prey with their sensitive beaks.

Greater flamingo
The greater flamingo stands up to 1.2 m tall and is one of the strangest birds with its spindly legs, long neck and peculiar bent beak. The beak works as a sieve to filter tiny animals like shrimps from the water, as the flamingo swishes it from side to side in a shallow lagoon.

Boat-billed heron
Most herons have long, thin, pointed beaks. The boat-billed heron has a broad, flattened beak like the hull (body) of a ship. This heron is not quick enough to stab fish or frogs. Instead it scoops its broad beak through the water to catch little shrimps, grubs and other small, slow-moving animals.

Maguari stork
The Maguari stork lives on the pampas – the wide, open grasslands of Argentina and nearby countries in South America. It eats mainly insects.

Bald ibis
This ibis lives in dry scrub and nests on cliffs. It has become rare in recent years. This may be due to its habitat becoming even drier, partly due.to water being pumped away for farmland.

Yellow-billed stork
A common waterbird in Africa, especially in eastern parts, the yellow-billed stork lives on lakes, marshes and sometimes on coasts. Like certain other storks and also the bald ibis, it has bare skin around its face. Otherwise its face feathers would get wet and dirty while feeding.

Hammerkop
The hammerkop from Africa is a strange relative of the storks. Its name means 'hammerhead' because its thick beak and the feathers on the back of its head make it look like the end of a hammer. Its nest is also unusual – a huge, untidy dome up to 2 m high. The nest may take almost six weeks to construct.

Royal spoonbill
Found in Australia, New Zealand and New Guinea, royal spoonbills build big stick nests in tall trees near water. They wade in the shallows to catch small prey.

One huge member of the stork group, the marabou stork of Africa, has the longest wings of almost any land bird. They are more than 3 m from tip to tip.

Storks, herons and similar waterbirds

Royal birds of open waters

Swans are the largest waterfowl and some of the heaviest flying birds. They need a long stretch of open water to take off, running across the surface as they pick up speed. Once in the air they are powerful fliers and some types cover huge distances each year on migration. A swan has a long, flexible neck to stretch almost 100 cm down into the water when feeding. Because of the swan's large size, strength, beauty and grace it has featured in many myths and legends. Swans have also inspired artists, writers and musicians for centuries and are often called 'royal' birds. Some types, like mute swans, are tame and live on busy lakes and rivers.

20

Whooper swan

Whooper swans are very similar to trumpeter swans except for the bright yellow triangular patch on the beak. They live across Europe and Asia, breeding in northern areas like Iceland, Scandinavia and northern Russia. They migrate to spend the winter farther south in Western and Eastern Europe.

Black-necked swan

This swan is found in South America and is particularly common in Argentina and Brazil. It prefers marshes and shallow water to deeper rivers and lakes. Flocks of black-necked swans sometimes rest on the sea just offshore, bobbing up and down one behind another in a long line.

Whistling swan

Whistling swans are the North American variety of the swan species called the tundra swan. Another variety of the same species is Bewick's swan of Asia and Europe. Both varieties are small for swans. Yet they fly huge distances from their Arctic breeding places for winter on coasts and marshes to the south.

Australian black swan

Most swans are white. Australian black swans are not. They have been taken to lakes and ponds around the world as a dark, contrasting addition to the local white swans. In their original home of Australia black swans breed in large colonies and often form huge flocks.

Mute swan

Mute means silent, but the mute swan is not. It makes various grunts and hissing noises. However it does not have the musical calls of many other swans which are named after the sounds they make, like the whistler and trumpeter. In flight the wings of the mute swan beat powerfully and slowly with a swishing sound.

Trumpeter swan

A North American swan that certainly lives up to its name, its loud, bugle-like cries carry over great distances. Trumpeters breed mainly in the far north of North America, especially Alaska. They move south for the winter but not very far, to the open water along Canadian coasts and on large lakes in national parks.

The mute swan is one of the heaviest of all flying birds, weighing up to 18 kg. It usually needs at least 50 m of open water for take-off and landing.

Swans

Honking, walking and pecking

22

Geese are between swans and ducks in size, and they spend much time walking about and feeding on the ground. In spring they fly north to breed on the icy, treeless plains called the tundra that surround the Arctic Ocean. During the long days of summer food is plentiful here. But the summer only lasts a few weeks, so in early autumn the geese fly south back to warmer regions. These long seasonal journeys are called migrations. For the winter the geese live near lakes, rivers, estuaries and coasts. They often form large, honking flocks as they waddle steadily across marshes and fields, pecking for food. Sometimes they damage farm crops.

Canada goose
As its name suggests, the Canada goose came originally from North America. But it has spread to Britain and northern Europe, where it is familiar as a semi-tame bird in parks, gardens and farmyards. It is one of the largest geese, and its long neck gives it a swan-like appearance in flight.

Red-breasted goose
This very colourful goose breeds in Siberia. It builds its nest and rears its goslings near to the nest of a bird of prey such as a rough-legged buzzard. The buzzard might attack the chicks. But the risk is worth it, since the buzzard also keeps away Arctic foxes who are more likely to eat the goslings.

Emperor goose
These small, stocky geese breed around the coasts of the Bering Sea, where the far east of Russia is within sight of Alaska in North America. They like to nest on coastal marshes and tundra. In the winter the emperor goose sometimes wanders as far south as the warm coasts of California.

Brent goose
Known as the brant goose in North America, this is a small and active member of the group with dark plumage. It prefers coastal areas with mud flats and salt marshes rather than inland regions, and it sits and bobs on the sea like a duck. The Brent goose especially likes to eat seaweeds and eelgrass.

Barnacle goose
Barnacle geese are very noisy, making barks and yaps that sound like small dogs fighting. They breed mainly in Greenland and Svalbard (Spitsbergen). Before people discovered such remote nesting areas, they thought these geese hatched from the barnacles that grow on boats and driftwood.

Snow goose
Snow geese are well named from their almost pure white feathers. A flock of thousands of these beautiful birds can look like a snowstorm. Snow geese nest in the Arctic in the far north of North America, laying eggs even before the snow melts. They migrate to the coasts farther south for the winter.

Geese are sometimes kept as 'guard birds'. They honk loudly, flap their wings and peck anyone who seems suspicious. They also honk at cars and other vehicles.

Dabbling, dipping and diving

Few rivers and lakes around the world are without ducks – the most common and familiar of all waterbirds (waterfowl). A duck spends much of its time swimming and so it has a light, buoyant body with a thick layer of waterproof feathers, and webbed feet to push itself along the surface or swim beneath. The dabbling or dipping ducks are the largest duck group. They dabble their beaks at the surface or 'up-end' so the head and neck are under the water with the tail pointing straight up into the air. Dabblers include the mallard, wigeon, gadwall and teal. Other ducks, such as the pochard and tufted duck, dive and swim deeper under the water to feed.

Hooded merganser
The male hooded merganser has a shiny green head and neck, and a fan-like crest. This American duck raises its young in tree holes.

Barrow's goldeneye
This diving duck breeds in North America and Iceland, in tree holes or rocky crevices. The male's glossy purple head makes his bright yellow eyes stand out.

Common scoter
Scoters are ducks of the open ocean, gathering there in winter flocks. They nest on small inland lakes but soon return to sea with their just-hatched chicks.

Ruddy duck
North and South America are the ruddy duck's original home. But it has been taken to brighten up the waterways of Britain and is spreading there. The ruddy duck has a stiff tail held up at an angle. The male's courtship display involves rapid paddling as he holds his head against his chest.

Wigeon
Wigeons are often seen flapping and wheeling in flocks over wetlands, making their characteristic whistling calls. These ducks feed more like geese, pecking at plants as they waddle through meadows and marshes. The male has delicately patterned plumage with a pale cap or crown on the head.

Cinnamon teal
This duck lives on marshes, lakes and ponds in western North America. It is named from the glowing, rusty-red shades of the feathers on the head and body of the male, or drake. He also has bright, striped-looking wings folded along his back. But the female, as in most ducks, is dull mottled brown.

Surf scoter
The surf scoter is larger and has a thicker, stronger beak compared to the common scoter. It is a North American duck and has distinctive white patches on its head. Surf scoters nest in the northern woods of Canada. Then, as their name suggests, they move to coastal seas for the rest of the year.

Many ducks quack but the hooded merganser is one of the world's quietest birds. Only the male makes a noise, which is a throaty purr like a cat – and then only at breeding time.

Kings of the bird world

26

Eagles are among the biggest, strongest and fiercest birds in the world. Like other raptors (birds of prey) they have powerful feet and talons (claws) for seizing victims and sharp, hooked beaks for tearing flesh. Their large eyes can spot prey many kilometres away. But most eagles are difficult to spot themselves because they are wary and live in remote places like islands, mountains and thick forest. Smaller eagles take mice and voles. Medium-sized types swoop on rabbits. Fish and sea eagles have extra-curved talons and rough toe skin to grasp their slippery meals. The largest eagles carry away monkeys, small deer and hares.

Steller's sea eagle

One of the most powerful of all birds, this eagle has a wingspan of 2.4 m and a massive beak to rip the flesh from fish, dead seals and beached whales. Steller's sea eagles breed around the Bering Sea between Asia and North America. They often gather off the island of Hokkaido, Japan.

Crested serpent eagle

This small eagle is widespread across Southeast Asia. But it is seldom seen since it tends to hunt from the cover of the forest, suddenly swooping from a tree to surprise its victim. As the name suggests, this eagle has a head crest of feathers and it hunts snakes and lizards as well as the usual prey.

White-bellied sea eagle

This small sea eagle lives from India across to Australia. It soars over the water and glides down to grab a fish just under the surface.

Australian little eagle

The little eagle of Australia and New Guinea has long, feathered legs and a short crest on its upper neck. It hunts a wide range of prey including worms.

Spanish imperial eagle

A rare bird from central and southern Spain, this eagle favours mixed habitats with forest, scrub and marsh or lakeside.

Bonelli's eagle

Forest and scrub for hunting, with cliffs nearby for nesting, are the favoured home of Bonelli's eagle. It soars over hillsides and valleys, watching carefully for prey below – mainly small mammals and ground birds. Sadly Bonelli's eagle is becoming rare. It still survives in remote parts of Spain.

Philippine eagle

Truly huge at 90 cm from beak to tail, this great bird equals the harpy as the world's biggest eagle. Despite its size and power it is agile enough to pluck monkeys from tropical forest tree tops. A threatened species, only a few hundred of these eagles survive in the mountains of certain Philippine islands.

The bald eagle, the national bird of the USA, is a kind of fish eagle – and is not bald at all. However from a distance its white head feathers make its head look bare.

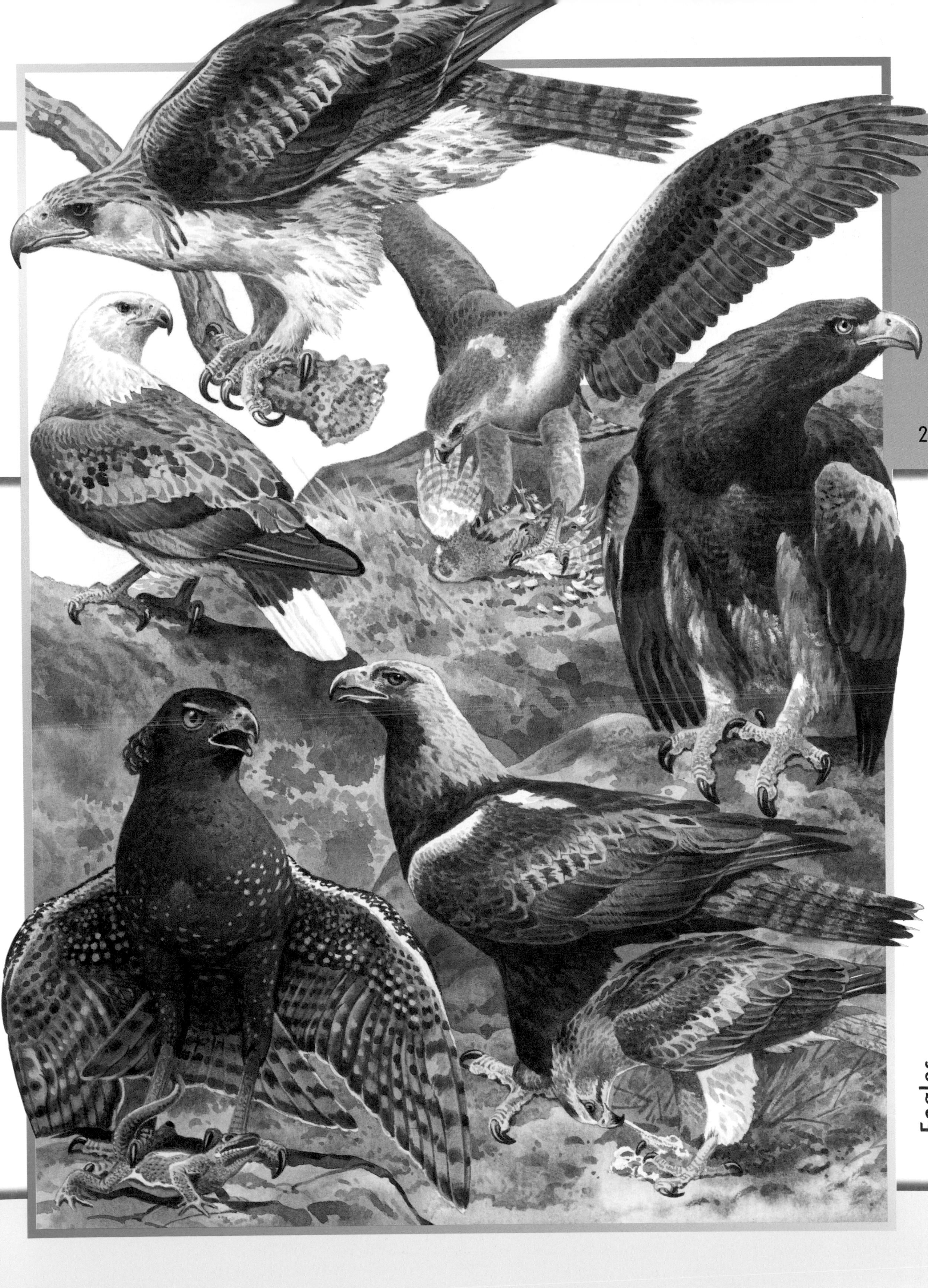

Flying death on fast wings

28

Falcons are fast-flying birds of prey. They use speed to chase and catch victims, twisting and turning with amazing aerobatic skill. Large falcons hunt mainly other birds, up to the size of pigeons and partridges. Some of these big and powerful falcons, like the peregrine and saker, are almost the equal of eagles. They swoop and thud their talons into the victim in mid air, in a blur of feathers and blood. Smaller falcons tend to prey on little songbirds and also on large flying insects such as dragonflies, butterflies and beetles. Kestrels hunt by hovering into the wind, head perfectly still and staring at the ground, before diving to pounce on their prey.

Red-legged falconet
This dainty bird is common in open forests that cover the foothills of the Himalaya Mountains and stretch across to Southeast Asia. Falconets are the smallest birds of prey. The red-legged falconet is only 18 cm from beak tip to tail end. Its legs are not red but the feathers just above are.

Red-headed falcon
The striking chestnut-red cap of this bird contrasts with the mainly grey plumage and barred chest as seen in other members of the group. The red-headed falcon is commonest in parts of East Africa. It often nests in palm trees and it feeds mainly on other birds, which it tears up for its chicks.

Barred forest falcon
Found from Mexico through Central America to Argentina, this falcon feeds mainly on lizards and snakes, small birds and mammals such as rats and mice. It has a long tail and short, rounded wings so it can swerve and turn at speed among the close trees of its dense woodland home.

Eleonora's falcon
This long-winged falcon specializes in hunting small birds. It breeds unusually late in the summer, in colonies on rocky islands in the Mediterranean Sea. This late breeding enables the falcon to catch many of the small songbirds flying past, heading south for winter, to feed its own chicks.

Laughing falcon
This falcon's loud, repeated two-part call sounds slightly like the 'ha-ha!' of human laughter. The rainforests of Central and South America are its home, where it catches mainly snakes – including poisonous ones. The falcon's armoured talons (clawed toes) strike too fast for the snake to bite back.

Saker falcon
One of the largest and most powerful falcons, the saker is a bird of open country, especially dry scrub and steppe (grassland). It is found from eastern Europe across Central Asia to China. This majestic hunter seizes ground-living mammals like hares, marmots and pikas as well as other birds.

The peregrine falcon is the world's fastest-moving animal, reaching more than 250 km/h in its power-dive called the 'stoop'.

Falcons

Plump, game and colourful

Gamebirds are mostly large, plump-bodied and spend much time on the ground. They are known as 'game' because they were hunted for their tasty meat, and still are in some regions. The group includes pheasants, grouse, partridges, snowcocks, francolins, quails, turkeys, guinea fowl and guans. The pheasants in particular have amazing plumage – especially the males (cocks) at breeding time. Their long, flowing feathers are beautifully patterned in dazzling shades of blue, red, green and gold to attract a mate. The females (hens) tend to have drab brown plumage for camouflage. It is their job to build the nest, sit on the eggs and tend to the chicks.

Argus pheasant
The male argus pheasant of Southeast Asia has very long, ornamental wing feathers to impress his possible breeding partners. He prepares a special arena in a forest clearing by moving leaves and plants. Then he calls to the females before beginning his leaping, dancing courtship display.

Swinhoe's pheasant
A rare species, Swinhoe's pheasant is found in the wild only on the island of Taiwan, like the mikado pheasant. This gamebird is small and delicate compared to other pheasants. It has suffered through loss of its habitat in recent years, as its tropical forest home is destroyed.

Mikado pheasant
This pheasant is very rare and now protected by law on its home island of Taiwan in East Asia. A special reserve has been created to protect both it and Swinhoe's pheasant. In many areas pheasant eggs and chicks are eaten by introduced animals such as cats and rats.

Indian peafowl
The massive tail fan of the male or peacock is one of nature's most spectacular sights. It is covered in eye-like spots and the huge feathers quiver and rattle during his courtship display for the female or peahen. The peafowl's home was India and nearby countries but it has now spread around the world.

Turkey
The wild turkey of North America lives in forest and scrub, where it feeds on the ground eating seeds, nuts and berries. At night it flaps into the branches to rest. The various kinds of farmyard turkeys, popular food at events such as Christmas and Thanksgiving, have been bred from this wild relative.

Golden pheasant
Like many of its pheasant relatives, the golden pheasant is often kept in bird collections for the male's beautiful plumage. This gamebird came originally from the forests of China. During courtship the cock spreads the fan-like feathers at the sides of his head to cover his face and beak.

The world's most colourful and shiniest bird is the Himalayan monal pheasant, with glistening feathers in shades of blue, green, purple and orange.

Pheasants, peafowl and turkeys

At the water's edge

Waders are truly shore birds, specialized for feeding at the water's edge. Most live along the mud flats, salt marshes, beaches and rocky coasts of the sea but some are found near lakes, ponds and marshes inland. A typical wader has long, thin legs to walk in shallow water without getting its feathers wet, and a long, thin beak to jab and probe in soft mud or sand for worms, shellfish and other small creatures. Some waders have shorter beaks and peck rapidly for tiny creatures on the surface. Many waders breed in the Arctic during the brief summer, then travel or migrate south to spend the winter along the shores of milder regions.

32

Redshank
One of Europe's commonest waders, the redshank really does have bright orange-red legs – and a beak to match. It nests on high, boggy moors and coasts.

Black-tailed godwit
This large wader breeds on marshes in Europe and Asia. Its long bill can probe deep into damp soil to pull out worms and grubs.

Common sandpiper
An active bird of rivers and lakes, the common sandpiper stands on a waterside boulder and bobs its head up and down as it feeds. It is a small and very shy wader. If disturbed it flits away quickly, low across the water's surface, making its high-pitched 'twee-wee-wee' alarm call.

Oystercatcher
The oystercatcher uses its strong, chisel-shaped bill to hammer into mussels and oysters. It levers open the shell parts to get at the soft flesh inside. It can also crack open crabs and sea snails.

Avocet
The avocet's beak has a unusual upward curve. The bird swishes it from side to side while holding it at the surface or just under the water, to filter out its food of tiny animals.

Curlew
One of the biggest waders, the curlew uses its long, down-curved bill to extract grubs and worms from deep in soil, sand and mud. Curlews often gather on the mud flats of an estuary (river mouth). As they wheel across the sky they make their flight call which is a sad, lonely-sounding, rising whistle: 'coor-lee'.

Stone curlew
The stone curlew is an unusual wader in two ways. It is found in dry, sandy or stony places like heaths and moors. It is also active at twilight and night.

Lapwing
The lapwing looks black and white at a distance, but has beautiful glossy green and purple upper parts. It often walks across farmland pecking for soil animals.

The oystercatcher's beak is so strong that it can break open most kinds of shelled animals, including crabs and snails. It can even knock limpets off rocks.

Waders

Stocky seabirds with paddle wings

Auks are plump, stocky, upright, waddling seabirds – the northern versions of the penguins which live in the far south, in Antarctica. Unlike penguins, auks have not lost the power of flight. But their wings are only just large enough to keep them in the air, and they have to flap very fast to stay aloft. This is because an auk's wings are also adapted as paddles for swimming and diving, to hunt for fish beneath the waves. The squat body and thick layers of tight-packed feathers keep in body warmth and keep out the cold waters of the northern seas. Auks breed on seaside cliffs and ledges where most predators cannot reach their eggs or chicks.

Atlantic puffin
The puffin's deep, narrow beak has very sharp edges to hold several fish at once. The beak's colour is much brighter in spring to attract a breeding mate.

Little auk
These starling-sized seabirds breed in their millions on rocky slopes around Greenland, Iceland and Svalbard. They feed on tiny animals like shrimps.

Brunnich's guillemot
This auk stays in the cold waters of the far north even in winter. Its main plumage is so dark brown that from a distance it looks black.

Horned puffin
The horned puffin has an even more massive bill than its Atlantic cousin. In summer it breeds along the coasts of Alaska, then it flies as far south as California for a warmer winter.

Razorbill
Razorbills are found around the coasts of the North Atlantic Ocean. The sharp-edged and sharply-hooked beak is well named since it can easily slash or peck through human skin.

Guillemot
Unlike Brunnich's guillemot, this bird flies south in winter from the coldest Arctic seas. It dives under the surface to catch fish, worms and shellfish. Its single egg is laid on a bare cliff ledge.

Black guillemot
This auk stays close to shore, where it dives deep after fish. In winter its plumage changes from mainly black to largely white and it almost looks like a gull.

Crested auklet
This auk lives on the Aleutian Islands in the North Pacific between Alaska and Russia. The curved crest is larger in summer to impress a mate during courtship.

Tufted puffin
The huge red and yellow bill looks even more extraordinary with the yellow head feathers curving back from behind each eye.

The biggest auk, known as the great auk, could not fly. It was killed by sailors for its meat, eggs and feathers. Great auks died out for ever in 1844.

Auk seabirds

Colourful, curious and clever

Parrots are lively, inquisitive and intelligent – for birds. The group includes cockatoos, parakeets, lovebirds, macaws, conures and lories (lorikeets). A typical parrot has colourful feathers, a large head, big beady eyes and a strong, hooked beak to crush even the hardest seeds. The beak is also used as an extra foot to clamber about in trees. Parrots make many calls and some mimic other sounds, including the human voice. The combination of colour, inquisitive behaviour, copying our speech, the ability to learn tricks, and being long-lived have all made parrots popular pets. But many are still illegally captured and several types are endangered.

Palm cockatoo
Unusually dark for a cockatoo, this large species has a tall head crest and huge bill to crack open even extremely hard palm nuts and similar seeds. It inhabits tropical forests.

Gang-gang cockatoo
This male of this small grey cockatoo species makes a call like a rusty, creaking gate hinge. In the breeding season he also has a bright red head.

Sulphur-crested cockatoo
This large yellow-crested bird forms flocks to feed on seeds and fruit. It is seen in parks and gardens in north and east Australia and soon becomes tame at the bird table.

Long-billed corella
This cockatoo is unusual because it spends much time on the ground, digging for roots with its long, strong, pale beak.

Hyacinth macaw
The world's largest parrot, from tropical South America, this massive macaw is under threat from unlawful collecting.

Pink cockatoo
The white plumage of this tropical bird is 'shot through with soft pink flush'. Its head crest displays bands of scarlet and yellow when spread.

Kea
The kea is named after its piercing call. It lives in New Zealand and uses its long upper beak to tear flesh from fruits – and to rip flesh off dead animals.

Yellow-tailed black cockatoo
Dark except for its long, yellow-edged tail and yellow cheeks, this parrot from Tasmania and south-east Australia has a weird wailing call.

Red-tailed black cockatoo
These noisy birds gather in flocks of 200 or more. The scarlet patches on the tail shine brightly as the cockatoo flaps along slowly.

Parrots are among the longest-lived of all birds. Larger kinds reach 40–50 years of age. In captivity some have lived for more than 80 years.

Parrots, cockatoos and macaws

Birds with babysitters

38

The 127 members of the cuckoo family are spread all over the world. But not all of them sing 'cuck-ooo!' and lay their eggs in other birds' nests. Most cuckoos in Europe, Africa and Asia do – they are brood parasites. The female places each of her eggs in the nest of another pair of birds. The new parents do not notice the extra egg and so become unknowing 'babysitters', feeding and raising the hungry chick. Across the ocean in the Americas, most cuckoos build their own nests and care for their own chicks in the usual way. Coucals are types of cuckoos that live mainly in Africa and Asia, on the ground or in the low bushes of scrubby countryside.

Hoatzin
One of the world's strangest birds, the hoatzin dwells in the Amazon's densest swamps. It is about the size of a chicken, eats only plant food and flies weakly, preferring to clamber through the branches. The hoatzin chick has finger-claws on its wings to help it climb – a feature found in no other living bird.

Purple-crested turaco
Turacos are close relatives of cuckoos but live only in Africa. They eat almost entirely fruits, including berries that would quickly poison most animals (and people). Other birds give their growing young at least some meat in the shape of grubs, slugs and worms. Yet turaco chicks are fed mostly fruits.

Great spotted cuckoo
This cuckoo lays its eggs in other birds' nests, but the chick is not quite as violent as in other cuckoos. It does not tip out the unhatched eggs and chicks of the parent bird. But it does eat most of the food that they bring. Also, being so big and strong, it may lean on the other chicks and squash them to death.

Red-billed cuckoo
The red-billed cuckoo of Southeast Asian rainforests stays mainly on the ground and is strong enough to tackle mice and lizards. Like most cuckoos it can fly and run well but is not a great climber. It has the typically powerful, partly hooked cuckoo beak for grabbing all kinds of food.

Senegal coucal
Locusts, beetles, mice, frogs and the chicks of other birds are all tasty meals for this cuckoo. Its odd call sounds like water bubbling from a spring.

Common coucal
Common indeed, this adaptable coucal can survive on a wide variety of food in forests, grassland and farmland. Its call is 'boob-boob-boob'.

Didric cuckoo
Instead of 'cuck-ooo' this African member of the family sings 'dee-derr-rik', which has become its first name. It clings to tree trunks and pecks at the bark for grubs and caterpillars.

If a pair of small birds like warblers raise a cuckoo chick, the 'baby' grows to be 10 times the size of the parents!

Cuckoos and coucals

Silent flight, hunters at night

Owls are the specialist night hunters of the bird world. They catch mainly small animals like mice, voles and lizards, although larger owls prey on rabbits and birds (including other owls) while smaller types hunt moths, beetles and other little creatures. The fishing owls of Africa and Asia grab fish, frogs and crayfish from shallow water using their long, unfeathered legs and sharp 'fish-hook' claws. The owl's wing feathers have soft edges which means they are almost totally silent in flight, so the owl can swoop undetected on its prey. Huge eyes give the owl good night vision, but its hearing is even better – four times more sensitive than the ears of a cat.

African wood-owl
This medium-sized owl is common in south and east Africa. But unlike many owls that hunt at dusk, it only comes out in darkness, and so it is heard but rarely seen.

Barking owl
The growls and barks of this owl are eerily dog-like. In New Guinea and Australian forests it eats opossums as well as the usual owl prey.

Papuan hawk-owl
This rare owl lives in New Guinea forests where logging is a major threat. It has a hawk-like long tail and rounded wings.

Malay eagle owl
Eagle owls are among the largest owls. Some have wingspans of 1.5 m. The Malay eagle owl is slightly smaller but still a powerful hunter, recognized by its very long 'ear tufts'. (These are not real ears but simply long feathers.) Its mysterious hooting, groaning calls are said to be made by demons of the night!

White-faced scops owl
The ghostly black-rimmed white face and long 'ear tufts' of this African owl make it one of the most distinctive members of the family. Its favourite hunting method is to sit and wait on a tree branch, then drop silently onto a passing victim below – a mouse, an insect or even a scorpion.

Elf owl
Only 12 cm long, this tiny owl from southern North America is one of the smallest owls. In its desert habitat it nests in old woodpecker holes in the giant saguaro cactus.

Seychelles scops owl
Known only from one island in the Seychelles, this small owl inhabits old forests on mountain slopes. It has a call like a clock's tick-tock.

Burrowing owl
Small and long-legged, this owl lives in grasslands throughout the Americas. It digs its own burrow or takes over one from a rabbit or prairie dog.

The barn owl is the most widespread bird in the world. It is found on every continent (except Antarctica) and in almost every habitat from remote mountains to busy towns.

Wide-mouthed night hunters

Nightjars are big-eyed, fluffy-looking, graceful fliers with some of the best camouflage in the bird world. Their mottled grey-brown plumage makes them almost impossible to spot as they sit perfectly still by day, among leaves and twigs on the ground or in a tree. At night they glide through the dark, snapping up moths and similar insects in their gaping mouths. Frogmouths are close cousins of nightjars, and as their name suggests, they too have wide, gaping mouths. They also fly at night but are less agile than nightjars, diving down from a perch to catch prey on the ground. Many of these birds have strange calls that sound like engines or machines.

Guachero
The guachero of Central and South America is a close relative of nightjars. It is unusual in many ways. It spends all day deep in a cave, then comes out at night to feed on very oily fruits. The guachero finds its way in total darkness by making loud clicks and hearing the bounced-back echoes – just like a bat.

Common potoo
Potoos are named after their calls and are in the same bird group as nightjars. The common potoo of Central America is another bird with incredible camouflage. When alarmed it stretches upwards on its perch and goes very stiff, so that it looks just like an extra piece of broken branch.

Tawny frogmouth
The tawny frogmouth's plumage blends perfectly with its background as it sits on a tree, looking exactly like an old bark-covered stump. This frogmouth is found in Australia and is large enough to swoop down onto mice and lizards, which it tears up with its strong, hooked beak.

Standard-winged nightjar
The 'standards' of this bird's name are two enormously long wing feathers which may stretch for 50 cm. The courtship flight of this nightjar, which lives in Africa, is very spectacular. As the male flies slowly in circles, his long feathers trail behind like a miniature airplane towing a display banner.

Pennant-winged nightjar
A bird of Central and southern Africa, this nightjar has a long, trailing plume on each wing. The plumes may be twice as long as the bird itself. Only the end of the plume is feathered. Most of it is the wire-like shaft. As in similar nightjars, the male uses them to impress the female.

Whip-poor-will
An American type of nightjar, the whip poor-will is named after its call. This can be repeated so often for so long that it becomes very irritating to human listeners! The whip-poor-will is fairly common in conifer and mixed broadleaved woods. It hunts close to the ground, snapping up large insects.

The nightjar's song does not sound like a bird at all, but like the chugging of a distant motorbike.

Nightjars, frogmouths and potoos

Tiny, brilliant masters of the air

44

The Amazon region teems with tiny, brilliantly coloured birds that dart among the leaves like feathered jewels. They flap so fast, their wings look like a blur and sound like a low droning buzz or hum. These are the hummingbirds. Most can dash forward at great speed yet stop on a dot to hover in mid air, and then fly backwards or even straight up like a miniature rocket. No other birds are so speedy and aerobatic – except perhaps for their close cousins, the swifts. The common swift spends more time in the air than almost any bird except the great albatross. It feeds, courts, mates, rests and even sleeps on the wing.

Sword-billed hummingbird

Most hummingbirds have long beaks to probe into flowers, and long tube-shaped tongues to sip and suck the nectar. The sword-billed has the longest beak compared to its body size of any bird. It not only reaches into the deepest funnel-shaped flowers but also pecks up small insects hiding there.

Crimson topaz

In the Amazon rainforest a crimson topaz darts across a sunlit clearing. Its two black tail feathers trail behind. It's a male impressing his mate. The female lacks tail streamers but she too has glittering plumage. She differs from most female hummingbirds, which are duller than males for camouflage when nesting.

Popelaire's thornbill

Thornbill hummingbirds live mainly in the cooler forests on the slopes of the Andes Mountains. They sip up nectar and also snap up small grubs, beetles and similar creatures. The speed of flapping is average for a hummingbird at about 50 wing beats per second.

Frilled coquette

Normally shy and hidden by leaves, frilled coquettes forget their secretive habits at breeding time. Female and male resemble butterflies as they flutter and dance in mid air. Like all hummingbirds they feed mainly on sweet, sugary flower nectar. Only this has enough energy to power their fast-flying lifestyle.

Ruby-throated hummingbird

Only the male has the glowing throat colour – the female is white in this area. Ruby-throats are among the world's smallest migrating birds. On wings only 12 cm across they fly from summer breeding areas in eastern North America almost 1000 km to winter in Mexico, the Caribbean and Central America.

Common swift

The swift twitters and flits around trees, rocks, riverbanks and buildings as it catches gnats, midges and similar tiny flying insects. Swifts winter in Africa, then fly north and east to Europe and Asia to breed. Their feet are so small and weak that they can hardly perch on twigs, only cling to cliffs and walls.

Hummingbirds flap their wings faster than any other birds, more than 80 beats per second in some types.

Hummingbirds and swifts

Spear-fishing for a meal

46

With their bright plumage and rapid darting flight, kingfishers are well known but rarely seen. If disturbed they flash away with a whir of wings. Most feed on fish, as their name suggests, but some take insects, lizards, frogs and similar prey. The bird plunges like an arrow into the water and grabs the victim in its spear-like beak. Kingfishers nest in holes. Some dig their own tunnels in soft riverbanks. Others use hollow trees. Wood-hoopoes live only in Africa and use their long, curved beaks to gather insects from tree bark. Like the motmots of Central and South America and the todies of the Caribbean, they are close cousins of kingfishers.

Stork-billed kingfisher
This is one of the largest and most powerful kingfishers, reaching a bill-tip to tail-end length of 36 cm. It lives along wooded streams, lakes and paddies (flooded rice fields) in India and Southeast Asia. As well as catching fish, it includes insects, lizards and small birds in its diet.

Jamaican tody
Todies are tiny birds with mainly bright green plumage. Their hunting method is to sit and wait on a branch, then quickly fly into the open to grab a butterfly, beetle or similar insect flying past. Todies can hover in mid air almost as well as hummingbirds. This allows them to pick insects off leaves.

Black-capped kingfisher
A small kingfisher of river banks, rice fields and mangrove swamps, this species is found from India across Southeast Asia to the Philippines.

Malachite kingfisher
Common in parts of East and Central Africa, the malachite kingfisher's dazzling blue upper parts are set off by its long red beak.

Turquoise-browed motmot
This motmot lives in the steamy forests of Central America. Spoon-shaped tail feathers are a feature of the motmot group and are used to signal to other birds.

Cuckoo roller
This bulky, strong kingfisher is found in the forests and scrub of Madagascar. It feeds mainly on large insects and lizards high in the treetops.

Green wood-hoopoe
Wood-hoopoes are busy birds that cackle constantly as they flap through the trees. They poke their long bills into bark for insects.

Pied kingfisher
The pied kingfisher of Africa and Asia hovers over open water before plunging after fish. Pied kingfishers breed in groups and, unusually for birds, help each other to raise their chicks.

The biggest kingfisher rarely eats fish – but it does 'laugh' very loudly. It is the kookaburra of Australia and it preys on all kinds of small animals, even rats.

Rolling and tumbling

48

Bee-eaters are slim birds with bright feathers and long, down-curved beaks. Rollers are slightly larger, more stocky and crow-like, but they too have very colourful plumage. Members of both these groups are skilled, agile fliers. Bee-eaters twist and dart at speed as they chase after flying insects, including bees and wasps. The bird rubs or bashes the insect on a branch to remove the sting before eating it. Rollers are named from their spectacular courtship flights when they roll over and over, tumble and somersault in mid air to impress a mate. All the birds in these groups are found mainly in warmer regions, often in dry, sandy grassland or scrub.

Indian roller
It looks dark while stood on its perch, but in flight this roller reveals its dazzling blue wings and tail. It lives in South and East Asia and catches large insects, frogs and lizards.

European roller
A Mediterranean bird, this bulky roller often perches on telephone wires. It swoops down to the ground to catch beetles, crickets and similar large insects, also spiders.

Hoopoe
The hoopoe with its tall head crest cannot be confused with any other bird. It is often heard before it is seen, making the call which led to its name – a soft, three-note 'hoo-poo-poo'.

Red-bearded bee-eater
In the forests of Southeast Asia this large, heavy-bodied bee-eater picks insects from trees, rather than catching them in flight.

Blue-bellied roller
This distinctive roller has a blue-green, deeply forked, swallow-like tail. It inhabits open woodlands in Sudan and Uganda, in Africa.

Lilac-breasted roller
In East and Central Africa, this fine bird is recognized by its lilac chest and long tail streamers. It prefers open bush with isolated trees.

Red-throated bee-eater
Like many bee-eaters, this African type lives mainly in open grassland and savanna, seeking out river banks as nesting sites.

European bee-eater
Common in the Mediterranean area, this bee-eater is also seen in northern France. Favourite foods are bumblebees and dragonflies.

Carmine bee-eater
One of the largest and brightest bee-eaters, this type often rides on the backs of antelopes and cattle. It snaps up the insects they disturb.

To feed itself and its hungry chicks, a bee-eater must catch about 220 bees or similar insects each day. That's one every 4 minutes of daylight time!

Bee-eaters and rollers

Woodpeckers would peck wood

50

Most woodpeckers live up to their name and peck at trees with their chisel-shaped beaks, to find grubs and other small animals in bark and wood. They also chip out nesting holes in trunks. These activities help many other woodland birds, which come to feed under the loose bark or nest in old woodpecker holes. A woodpecker's foot has two toes pointing forwards and two backwards for an extra-secure grip when holding onto an upright tree trunk. Also the tail feathers are stiff and pointed so the woodpecker can lean back on them when climbing or hammering. And the bones and muscles in its head and neck are very strong, so it doesn't get a headache!

Acorn woodpecker
This woodpecker chips holes in trees and pushes acorns and other nuts into them, to eat when food is scarce in winter.

Red-collared woodpecker
The forests of south China and much of Southeast Asia are the haunts of this woodpecker. Its red neck collar is very distinctive.

White-backed woodpecker
A woodland bird from north-east Europe and Russia, this type likes forests with plenty of old, rotting trees and lakes or streams.

Orange-backed woodpecker
Like several woodpeckers this bird is often found by the loud tapping sounds it makes. It can pull or strip back large sections of bark to look for grubs underneath.

Gilded flicker
Flickers are large, common North American birds. They are bold and often seen in parks and gardens as well as in woodlands. The gilded flicker's underwings have a golden sheen.

White-bellied sapsucker
The sapsucker drills rows of holes in a tree, then licks up the sugary sap which oozes out using its brush-like tongue. It also gobbles up insects which feed on the sap.

Red-throated wryneck
Wrynecks resemble woodpeckers but lack stiff tail feathers. They twist their heads oddly to look around when alarmed, hence their name.

Greater yellow-naped woodpecker
Despite its colourful feathers, this woodpecker is hard to spot when it stands still in its forest home of eastern Asia.

Black-headed woodpecker
This noisy bird has a loud, squawking call in flight, when its bright red rump contrasts with the green body and red-capped black head.

A single green woodpecker may eat more than 2000 ants in one day.

51

Woodpeckers

Catching flies in mid air

52

The tyrant flycatchers are American birds, different from the flycatchers of Europe and Asia. With more than 400 kinds or species, they make up the largest family of birds in the Americas. Various tyrant flycatcher species are found from the conifer forests of northern Canada, down through North and Central America to the tip of South America. But the richest diversity is in the tropical rainforests of the Amazon region. As their name suggests, many of these birds chase and catch flies. Some of the larger types prey on creatures as large as crickets and lizards. A few tyrant flycatchers are brightly coloured but most species are fairly dull shades of brown or green.

Buff-breasted flycatcher
This rare bird lives in the dry, rocky canyons of Mexico and southern Arizona. It is very similar to the least flycatcher (shown just to its right in the illustration opposite). However the least flycatcher is much more common and lives in broadleaved woodlands across much of North America.

Black phoebe
The unusual combination of jet-black head, breast and upper body with a white belly area make this small, neat bird easy to identify. It is a common type of tyrant flycatcher in the dry woods of south-western North America. Like its relatives it has a fast, fluttering flight as it pursues small airborne insects.

Great crested flycatcher
With its crest and yellow belly, this is a common and distinctive bird of mixed woodlands, parks and gardens in eastern North America. In a wood it selects an old woodpecker hole or the natural cavity in a hollow tree for its nest site. It has also taken to nest boxes in gardens.

Superb lyrebird
Lyrebirds eat numerous kinds of foods. The superb lyrebird of south-east Australia shows off its amazing tail feathers during its courtship display, and makes a continuous stream of rich, tuneful sounds. It also copies the calls of local birds and even unnatural sounds like car sirens and chainsaws.

Vermilion flycatcher
The male vermilion flycatcher is named after his bright red plumage – red being an unusual colour in the flycatcher group. This colouring is mainly to attract a mate at breeding time. Female and young vermilion flycatchers are drab grey-brown which is much more suitable for camouflage.

Great kiskadee
This noisy bird is one of the largest of the group. Its thick, stout, all-purpose beak shows that it eats a wide range of foods, compared to the thin, delicate beaks of its cousins. As well as flies and other insects the great kiskadee hunts small mammals like mice, also frogs and lizards. It even dives for fish.

The eastern kingbird is one of the most aggressive birds. It readily attacks other birds that enter its territory, even much larger types such as crows and hawks.

Tyrant flycatchers

Small, bright, busy and noisy

Titmice (tits) are common garden birds with bright plumage and busy, acrobatic behaviour. They often hang under and clamber over bird-feeders and breed in garden nest-boxes. In America some types are known as chickadees. Bulbuls, another group of active songbirds, are larger than tits with bubbling, tuneful songs. They live mostly in Africa and southern Asia. Wrens are tiny, shy and skulk in thick bushes where their brown plumage makes them hard to see. But you can certainly hear them – for their size, wrens are the loudest of all birds.

54

Red-whiskered bulbul
Originally from India and Southeast Asia, this bulbul has been brought to new areas around Sydney, Australia and Miami, USA. It is tame and often comes to gardens.

Blue tit
Found in Europe, North Africa and Asia, this tit is one of the most common visitors at the bird table. Despite its small size it often chases much larger birds away from the food.

European wren
One of Europe's smallest birds, the wren is found in many habitats from open moor to dense marsh. It holds its tail almost upright and builds a domed nest among tree roots.

Long-tailed tit
Small and delicate, this tit builds an amazing melon-shaped nest from spiders' webs, moss and animal fur. The nest is lined with soft feathers.

Common iora
Found in India and Southeast Asia, the common iora is familiar in gardens and also lives in woods and mangrove swamps. It has a clear, whistling call.

Crested tit
The crested tit lives mainly in conifer woods, especially among pine or spruce trees. It eats the seeds from the cones as well as snapping up insects.

Golden-fronted leafbird
Named after its orange forehead, this bird hunts insects in the forest trees of South and Southeast Asia. It often copies other birds' calls.

Black-capped chickadee
One of the best-known garden birds in North America, this tit is named after its black head and 'chickadee' call.

Fairy bluebird
These bluebirds like to eat tropical fruits, especially figs. They are always on the move, hopping and flitting through forests in Southern Asia.

The tiny long-tailed tit gathers more than 2000 soft feathers to make its beautifully woven nest.

Tits, bulbuls and wrens

A bower for courtship

- Archbold's bowerbird
- Green (spotted) catbird
- Golden bowerbird (male and bower in background)
- MacGregor's (crested) gardener
- Tooth-billed bowerbird (tooth-billed catbird)

Bowerbirds are medium-sized, eat mainly fruit, and live in the forests of New Guinea and Australia. The male attracts or courts the female in an extraordinary way by building a bower. This varies according to the kind or species of bowerbird. It may be a simple mat of leaves and moss, or a pile of twigs, or a large and elaborate structure shaped like a tower, tent, maypole or walk-along 'avenue'. The male may even decorate and paint his bower with bright colours. He then dances, shows off his feathers and calls from his bower, to bring a female near. But the bower is not a nest. After mating the female leaves to build her nest in a bush and raise the chicks on her own.

Green catbird
Catbirds are types of bowerbirds but they do not build bowers. They are named from their miaowing, cat-like calls. (They are different from American catbirds, which are types of mockingbirds.) The green catbird of New Guinea and north-east Australia 'mews' at dawn, then forages among trees for fruits.

Golden bowerbird
The golden bowerbird's huge twig-and-stick bower is decorated with colourful mosses, flowers and fruits. It has a maypole-like shape. The finished structure may be as tall as a person! These bowerbirds live in a restricted area in the mountain tablelands of northern Queensland, Australia.

MacGregor's gardener
This bird builds a relatively simple bower. It consists of a vertical stick with twigs, stalks and similar decorations piled up around it. The final effect looks like a person-sized bottle-brush! The MacGregor's gardener is recognized by its thick head crest of golden-orange feathers.

Tooth-billed bowerbird
The dull browns of this Australian species make it hard to see in the forest. But it can be heard – its loud song includes sounds copied from other birds and animals like crickets. Its wavy-edged beak cuts off fresh leaves, both to eat and to decorate a clearing or 'stage' in the forest where the male courts.

Archbold's bowerbird
This bowerbird was discovered quite recently, in about 1940. It lives in mountain forests in New Guinea, at heights of up to 4000 m. Each male builds a mat of grasses and ferns, decorated with snail shells and the shiny wing cases of beetles. He then sings from a perch just above this bower.

LESS MEANS MORE
There are 18 species of bowerbirds. Those birds with the dull feathers build big, complicated bowers. They even decorate them with colourful petals, shells and berries, and smear on 'paint' of natural coloured juices. Males with the brightest plumage make smaller, simpler bowers.

Each type of bowerbird builds its own distinct bower. But young males make small, poorly crafted versions. Their bowers get bigger and better with experience over the years.

Bowerbirds and catbirds

Feathers fallen from paradise

58

European naturalists first ventured into the tropical forests of New Guinea in the late 18th century. They were so astonished by the incredible colours and shapes of the feathers that they believed the birds had 'fallen from paradise'. Each newly discovered species was named in honour of a European royal or noble person of the time, such as Princess Stephana, the King of Saxony and Count Raggi. In fact only males (shown here) display such amazing plumes, to impress partners at breeding time. Females are mostly drab brown or green for camouflage, since they must incubate (sit on and keep warm) the eggs and feed the chicks.

Blue bird of paradise
To attract his mate the blue bird of paradise hangs upside down from a twig, sprays out his wing and tail feathers and arches his two long tail plumes into an M shape. Then he sways to and fro and makes a courtship call that sounds like the cough and splutter of an old motorcycle engine.

King bird of paradise
Like the other 41 species in the bird of paradise group, the king lives mainly in rainforest. It feeds chiefly on fruits, along with some insects, frogs and other small animals. During his mating display the male holds out his wings and vibrates them like a fast-shaking fan.

Princess Stephana's bird of paradise
This bird of paradise is found unusually high for the group, up to 3000 m in the remote, cooler, cloud-forest mountains of south-west New Guinea. Most female birds of paradise lay two or three eggs, but the Princess Stephana female usually produces only one.

Raggiana bird of paradise
Many birds of paradise are threatened by felling of their rainforest homes for timber (the felling is sometimes done illegally). The Raggiana or Count Raggi's species copes with a wider range of habitats and has spread into scattered lowland woods and even rural gardens.

King of Saxony's bird of paradise
Many birds of paradise have long, ornate plumes (slim, ribbon-like feathers). But they are usually on the tail or wings. Only the King of Saxony's bird of paradise has them on the head. It is also one of the smaller types, only 22 cm from bill to tail tip (excluding the plumes).

Magnificent riflebird
Riflebirds are members of the bird of paradise group. This type is named after its popping, gun-like call. Like the Victoria riflebird, it lives in the rainforests of north-east Australia as well as New Guinea. Birds of paradise make a raucous squawking similar to their close cousins, the crows.

The magnificent riflebird is one of the few birds of paradise not named after a king, prince or similar titled person.

Birds of paradise

Squawking thieves

The crow family (see page 62) contains many large perching birds, including jays, magpies and nutcrackers. Many of the jays have bright, gaudy plumage and are easy to spot by sight – and by sound. But they are not famous for their beautiful songs. They make loud, hoarse, grating calls which sound like a person coughing with a sore throat! The birds use these harsh calls to keep contact with each other in woodland and scrub. Magpies and jays are adaptable eaters and take a very wide range of food, from seeds and nuts to insects, frogs and mice. They also steal the eggs and babies of other birds, which makes them pests in some regions.

60

Azure-winged magpie

This magpie is found in China and Japan – and, oddly, also halfway round the world in Portugal and Spain. It may have been brought back to Europe by exploring sailors returning from the Far East. Azure-winged magpies are very social, which means they form flocks with others of their kind.

Common jay

Jays live and breed mainly in mixed broadleaved woods across Europe and Asia. They have also spread into wooded parks and gardens, where they swoop between trees with a flash of their blue wing fronts and harsh calls. Like squirrels, jays often gather acorns and other nuts and bury them to eat later.

Turquoise jay

The Americas have more than 30 kinds of jays, mainly in the tropics. The turquoise jay is one of several threatened by loss of their forest home.

Blue jay

Common in woods and gardens across eastern North America, this jay feeds mainly on seeds and nuts. But it also raids birds' nests for eggs and chicks.

Nutcracker

Nutcrackers live in mixed woodland, from the uplands of Scandinavia across to the hills of eastern Europe. In autumn they gather piles of tree nuts and seeds, especially arolla pine.

Common magpie

Shiny black-and-white plumage and a long, green, glossy, blue-tipped tail are a magpie's main features. It prefers open country with trees and hedges and avoids thick woods. The female and male build a large twig nest high in a tree or bush. This has a loose, dome-shaped roof and a side entrance.

Plush-crested jay

The soft black feathers on the head of this jay form a crest which feels like a velvet cushion! Plush-crested jays live in forests in many parts of South America. Like several jays and magpies they copy the calls of other birds in their loud 'babble', and even imitate other animal sounds.

The plush-crested jay can mimic many sounds including frog croaks, monkey screeches and even (like parrots and mynahs) the spoken words of the human voice.

The cleverest birds?

Crows, rooks and ravens are found mainly in open country, including mountains, cliffs, moors and hillsides. Like their cousins the jays and magpies (see page 60) they are large, strong, adaptable birds with powerful beaks and legs, as much at home on the ground as in the air. Ravens are the largest members in the world of the huge group of birds known as perching birds (passerines). A raven is easily powerful enough to kill prey such as rabbits. Ravens and many crows tend to live on their own or with a breeding partner. Others like rooks, jackdaws and choughs lead more social lives. They roost and breed in colonies and feed together in flocks.

62

Raven
These massive corvids (members of the crow family) reach 65 cm in length. They can kill prey but usually scavenge on dead animals. In olden times they pecked at the bodies of criminals who had been hanged, so the raven became known as a bird of ill omen. Its deep, hollow call carries far over its upland home.

Rook
Rooks are similar to carrion crows except for a patch of pale skin at the beak base and feathered, shaggy-looking legs. Rooks also live mainly in groups whereas a crow tends to be alone. Rooks like open country with scattered fields and woods where they can find their main food of grubs, slugs and worms.

BRIGHT BIRD!
Crows and ravens use many tricks to gather food. Crows fly high with shellfish and drop them on rocks to crack them open. They wait near gull breeding colonies and dash in to steal unguarded chicks. Tests have shown that ravens can count up to five or six, outscoring birds like parrots.

Hooded crow
The hooded crow has a similar lifestyle to the all-black carrion crow but lives mainly in north, east and south-east Europe, also in north-west Scotland and Ireland. It prefers open hills and moors where it eats many foods from seeds to snails. Hooded and carrion crows may breed together.

Jackdaw
Jackdaws are noisy and active. They like to roost and breed in tree holes and on ledges along cliffs and rocky outcrops. Window ledges and chimney pots resemble these wild sites, which is why jackdaws have spread into towns and cities. They are also famous for 'stealing' shiny objects like coins and rings.

Chough
Choughs, with their distinctive red legs and red beaks, live in loose flocks. They are skilled, acrobatic fliers and utter high-pitched squealing calls. They live in rocky mountainous areas and along remote coasts in Europe. Choughs have become rare due to loss of the natural meadows where they feed on soil animals.

A flock of ravens is kept at the historic Tower of London in England. Legend says that if the ravens fly away, England will be taken over by invaders.

Crows, rooks and ravens

Index